DISCOVERING ANTARCTICA

Plants and Animals

June Loves

CHELSEA HOUSE
PUBLISHERS

A Haights Cross Communications Company

Philadelphia

This edition first published in 2003 in the United States of America by Chelsea House Publishers, a subsidiary of Haights Cross Communications.

Chelsea House Publishers
1974 Sproul Road, Suite 400
Broomall, PA 19008-0914

The Chelsea House world wide web address is www.chelseahouse.com

Library of Congress Cataloging-in-Publication Data Applied for.
ISBN 0-7910-7022-0

First published 1998 by
MACMILLAN EDUCATION AUSTRALIA PTY LTD
627 Chapel Street, South Yarra, Australia, 3141

Designed by Andrea Jaretzki
Cover design by Dimitrios Frangoulis
Typeset by Polar Design

Printed in China

Acknowledgements
The author would like to thank Rod Seppelt and Maria Turnbull of the Australian Antarctic Division for their assistance.

Cover: Graham Robertson/AUSCAPE

Bruce Cayboum/Hedgehog House, NZ/AUSCAPE, p. 29; Jean-Paul Ferrero/AUSCAPE, pp. 14, 15, 16, 22, 24 (bottom), 27 (bottom); International Photographic Library, p. 21 (bottom); Rod Ledingham, pp. 12, 19, 27 (top); Colin Monteath/AUSCAPE, pp. 5 (bottom), 11 (bottom); D. Parer & E. Parer-Cook/ AUSCAPE, p. 23, 28 (bottom); Doug Perrine/AUSCAPE, p. 20; The Photo Library, p. 4–5 © Julian Baum/SPL, 11 (top) © John Yates, p. 20; Graham Robertson/ AUSCAPE, pp. 5 (top), 18, 24 (top); Tui De Roy/AUSCAPE, pp. 6–7; Colin Monteath, Hedgehog House NZ/AUSCAPE, pp. 13, 17 (right), 25 (top), 28 (top); Kim Westerskov, Hedgehog House, NZ/AUSCAPE, p. 23 (bottom); Michael Whitehead/AUSCAPE, pp. 7, 10, 17 (left), 25 (bottom).

Words that appear in **bold type** can be found in the Glossary on pages 31 and 32.

Contents

Introduction

Antarctica is a huge continent that surrounds the **South Pole**. It is the fifth largest continent in the world. Like the Arctic regions in the north, most of Antarctica is covered in ice and snow for the entire year. In winter, the surrounding ocean also freezes, extending the area of the icy continent.

Because of the harsh climate, Antarctica has no trees and few plants. The largest land animal is a tiny **invertebrate** called a midge. Bigger animals, such as seals and penguins, live around the coast and on the **sub-Antarctic islands** nearby.

Many other animals and birds visit Antarctica and the sub-Antarctic islands during the short Antarctic summer, which lasts from November to January.

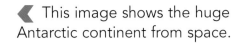 This image shows the huge Antarctic continent from space.

Emperor penguins are found in Antarctica. They live in groups called colonies, which can contain up to 100,000 birds.

Blue-eyed cormorants visit the sub-Antarctic islands during the short Antarctic summer.

Antarctic Plants

Only a few plants survive in Antarctica because of the extreme temperatures, fierce winds, and lack of rain.

Simple plants like algae, mosses, liverworts, and lichens can survive and grow in Antarctica. Many species of **microscopic** fungi are also found on the continent. There are about 20 different microscopic algae that grow in the snow. Other plants grow on the 2 percent of coastal rocky land that is free of ice.

Flowering Plants in Antarctica

Only two **species** of flowering plants are found in Antarctica.

▶ Lichens are well suited to Antarctica's freezing climate. They are common, colorful plants that grow in sheltered areas on stones, rocks, and in the soil.

▲ Algae are simple plants that take many forms. Snow algae may form brilliant red, yellow, or green patches on areas of **permanent** snow. Some blue-green and green algae live inside sandstone rocks.

Plant Life in Antarctic Lakes

A few species of plants, plankton, algae, and mosses live in and around Antarctica's freshwater and saltwater lakes. In Antarctica, many lakes with low salt levels have a thick covering of algae.

Antarctic Land Animals

Although birds, seals, and penguins are often seen in the Antarctic, the only land animals that live on Antarctica all year round are tiny. These animals are invertebrates, or animals without backbones. They include threadworms, wingless flies, and jumping insects. About 200 species have been discovered.

Invertebrates

Midges
Midges are the largest animals in Antarctica. The wingless midge grows to a length of one-half inch (12 millimeters) and is found only on the northern part of the Antarctic Peninsula.

Mites
Mites are the most common land animals in Antarctica. The majority of mites live mainly in Antarctic soil and vegetation. They are so small that the human eye can barely see them.

Protozoans
Protozoans are single-celled animals. Many live in **melt-water ponds**, Antarctic lakes, and in moist soil.

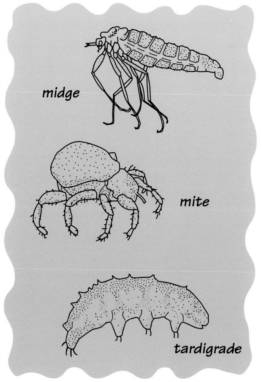

midge

mite

tardigrade

Tardigrades
Tardigrades are tiny, water-dwelling invertebrates that grow to less than one-thousandth of an inch (.25 millimeters) long.

Copepods
Copepods are tiny **crustaceans** that are related to shrimp. They live in the Antarctic lakes.

Antarctic Adaptation

Many of Antarctica's invertebrates avoid freezing by supercooling, or keeping their body temperatures below their normal freezing point.

Antarctic Food Webs

Food webs are part of every natural **habitat** and show what each animal eats. The food web in Antarctica is finely balanced. If any of the links are removed or harmed, the other animals in the web will be affected, too. Food webs can be affected by natural causes, such as unusual weather, or human causes, such as an oil spill or **overfishing**.

How the Antarctic Food Web Works

The oceans around Antarctica provide food that supports a huge number of birds, fish, **mammals**, and other animals.

Phytoplankton are the **primary producers** in Antarctic waters. They are the first link in the food web. They are tiny, simple plants such as algae. These plants bloom in spring and summer when the **pack ice** melts.

Phytoplankton are eaten by tiny animals called zooplankton and krill. Fish, penguins, seals, and whales then **prey** on krill. The fish and penguins in turn become food for other animals, such as toothed whales and leopard seals.

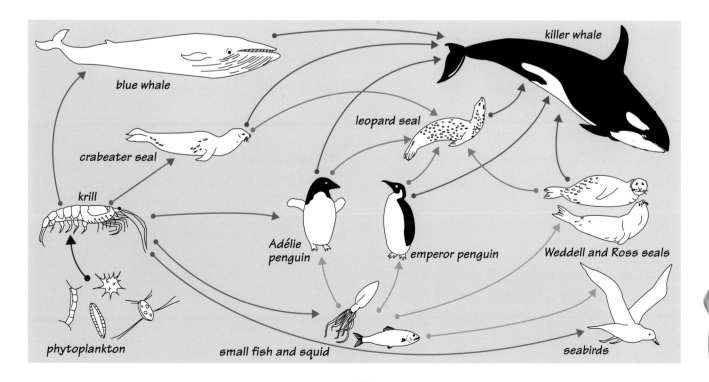

...als. They are common in Antarctic waters. ...al live in Antarctica. Weddell seals, Ross seals, ...and crabeater seals are found in Antarctic waters. The southern elephant seal and the Antarctic fur seal live mostly in the seas around the sub-Antarctic Islands.

◄ Seal pups are quite large at birth. Their most rapid growth is during the first few weeks of life, when they are drinking milk from their mother. By the second year, they have reached 50 to 80 percent of their adult length. The mother's milk supply is very **nutritious**.

Weddell Seals

Weddell seals are often seen in large groups on the **fast ice** along the coast. They are the best swimmers and can dive deeply. Weddell seals can stay underwater for more than one hour. During the long, dark winters they can survive under the ice where they scrape breathing holes with their teeth.

Facts about Weddell Seals
Food: fish, squid, and some crustaceans
Weight: 880 pounds (400 kilograms)
Length: 10 feet (3 meters)

Ross Seals

Ross seals are probably the rarest of Antarctica's seals, and little is known about them. They live on the coastal pack ice.

Facts about Ross Seals
Food: squid, fish, and krill
Weight: 440 pounds (200 kilograms)
Length: 7.5 feet (2.3 meters)

Leopard Seals

Leopard seals are strong, fast swimmers and ferocious hunters. They have powerful jaws and are often seen around penguin **rookeries** hunting for prey. Leopard seals are found on the pack ice and throughout the oceans surrounding Antarctica.

Facts about Leopard Seals
Food: penguins, young crabeater seals, and krill
Weight: 770 pounds (350 kilograms)
Length: 10 feet (3 meters)

▼ Leopard seals are named for their spotted skin.

▲ Crabeater seals are often seen lying on the **ice floes**.

Crabeater Seals

Crabeater seals are the most common Antarctic seals. They spend half their lives in the sea and on the pack ice. It is estimated that they make up half the world's seal population.

Facts about Crabeater Seals
Food: krill
Weight: 550 pounds (250 kilograms)
Length: 9 feet (2.7 meters)

11

Southern Elephant Seals

Southern elephant seals are the largest Antarctic seals and one of the largest of all mammals. Their name comes from the wrinkled sack of skin (called a proboscis) on top of an adult male's nose. This sack is like an elephant's trunk. The seals use this sack to make a deafening roar that scares away **rival** seals. Southern elephant seals **breed** on the sub-Antarctic islands and on islands off South Africa.

Male Southern Elephant Seals
Dominant southern elephant seal males have large **harems** of about 70 females. They spend many months defending their **territory** and harem from other males.

When **defensive**, the males will bellow, rear up, and puff up their proboscis to frighten off their enemies.

Pups
Southern elephant seal pups weigh up to 110 pounds (50 kilograms) at birth. Within the first two weeks of life, southern elephant seal pups may double their weight and begin to swim and hunt for themselves.

Facts about Southern Elephant Seals
Food: fish, squid, and crustaceans
Males   **Size:** 20 to 23 feet (6 to 7 meters) long
            Weight: up to 4.4 tons (4 metric tons)
Females **Size:** 11.5 feet (3.5 meters) long
            Weight: up to 1.1 tons (1 metric ton)

Antarctic Fur Seals

Antarctic fur seals are not true seals. They have ear flaps that can be seen and belong to the group of animals that includes sea lions.

The flippers of an Antarctic fur seal are very strong. As well as using them for swimming, they tuck their hind flippers under their bodies to move about quickly on land. Antarctic fur seals breed in harems. The main breeding population is on South Georgia, a sub-Antarctic island.

Facts about Fur Seals
Food: krill, squid, fish, and crustaceans
Male   **Size:** 6.5 feet (2 meters) long
            Weight: 220 pounds (100 kilograms)
Female   **Size:** 5 feet (1.5 meters) long
            Weight: 110 pounds (50 kilograms)

Antarctic fur seals have been hunted in the past for their fur and oil.

Penguins

Penguins are the most common birds in Antarctica. Although they do not fly, they are excellent swimmers. They spend most of their time in the water where they hunt krill and small fish. They only return to the ice and rocky coast to breed, **molt**, and grow new feathers.

Adaptations

Penguins are well **adapted** to the icy seas and freezing Antarctic conditions. Young penguins are born with fluffy down feathers, which they shed as they grow older. Adult penguins have a tightly packed outer layer of waterproof feathers that overlap an inner layer of soft down feathers. A thick layer of **blubber** between their skin and muscles acts as an **insulator** against the cold.

Penguins have a compact shape, which reduces the amount of body heat they lose. Penguins are also able to reduce the amount of blood that flows to their flippers and feet, which also saves body heat.

▶ Penguins live in large colonies called rookeries. A rookery may have thousands of penguins in it, which can make it a very noisy place. Female penguins lay one to two eggs in the rookeries during the breeding season.

Swimming

Penguins are good swimmers. They can dive up to 200 feet (60 meters) deep and swim up to 25 miles (40 kilometers) per hour.

Penguins use their wings to move quickly through the water. They steer with their feet and tails, which act as **rudders**. Penguins also use a restful swimming style that is similar to a dog paddling.

Camouflage

A penguin's black and white coloring helps it survive in the water. The white underside of a penguin blends with the light from above. This helps to protect penguins from **predators**, such as leopard seals.

Movement

A penguin's weight is distributed evenly over its legs. When it moves, it looks like a child just learning to walk. It uses its wings for balance.

Penguin Enemies

gull

killer whale

skua

leopard seal

giant petrel

Underwater Skills

Unlike most birds, penguins can stay underwater for more than 15 minutes. They sometimes jump out of the water like a porpoise, gulp some air, and then plunge back down again.

15

Types of Antarctic Penguins

The main types of penguins found in Antarctica and its surrounding islands are emperor, Adélie, gentoo, chinstrap, rockhopper, macaroni, king, and royal penguins.

⌃ Chinstrap penguins are named for the markings on their faces. They build nests on steep, rocky slopes.

⌄ Rockhopper penguins are the smallest penguins living close to Antarctica. They are so named because they hop from rock to rock. Rockhoppers use their beaks, wings, and sharp claws to help them climb. Instead of diving into the water like other penguins, they jump in feet first.

❮ Gentoo penguins are timid animals. They have orange-red beaks and white markings which look like a bonnet.

Adélie Penguins

Adélie penguins live on Antarctica and on some of the sub-Antarctic islands. It is estimated that they make up 50 percent of the penguin population in Antarctica.

Chicks

Adélie chicks have silver-gray down. One parent is always close by to protect them from enemies. When the chicks are about 3 weeks old, the adults leave them alone for the first time. Parents bring food for them back from the sea. They feed the chicks krill, small fish, squid, and crustaceans from their mouths.

Breeding

Adélie penguins live and breed on the shores of Antarctica as well as on some of the sub-Antarctic islands. They are the first birds to arrive on land in spring. The males arrive a few days before the females and start to build nests.

Incubation

An Adélie penguin usually lays two eggs. Incubation lasts about 35 days. The male fasts as it **incubates** the eggs, and the female returns to the sea to feed. When she returns, the female sits on the nest.

Movement

Adélie penguins make spectacular vertical jumps of up to 6.5 feet (2 meters) from the ocean to ice floes. They gain momentum from swimming quickly. This is a useful way to escape from leopard seals and other enemies.

Emperor Penguins

Emperor penguins are the largest and heaviest penguins. They have an average weight of 70 pounds (32 kilograms) and an average height of 4 feet (1.2 meters). They have bright yellow markings on their beaks, heads, and throats.

Breeding

Emperor penguins breed on the pack ice of Antarctica during the long, cold winter. They need nine months to complete their breeding season. They begin breeding in March. After mating, the female lays one egg in mid-May and then leaves to spend the rest of winter feeding at sea.

Incubation

Emperor penguins do not make nests. Instead, the male scoops the egg onto his feet, holding it under a fold of skin. He incubates the egg for about two months through freezing temperatures and blizzards of up to 124 miles (200 kilometers) per hour. During this time, he eats nothing and loses 40 percent of his body weight.

The huddling behavior of male emperor penguins saves up to 50 percent of the heat an individual bird would lose in a day.

Colonies

There are about 250,000 adult emperor penguins scattered around Antarctica. They live in groups called colonies, which contain from 300 to 100,000 birds.

Hatching

The females return from the ocean, fat from their feeding, just as the chicks are hatching. Each female recognizes her partner's voice from thousands of others. The chick is moved to the mother's feet so that the male may return to sea to hunt for his first food in two months.

It is often a two-day journey across 50 miles (80 kilometers) of pack ice to the open sea. The mother **regurgitates** fish to feed the chick.

After three weeks, the male returns to take over from the female. Soon the chicks will be big enough to be left in **creches** so both parents can bring food to them.

By mid-December, the chicks reach 60 percent of the adult body weight. They lose their fluffy down, develop sleek black and white feathers, and are ready to survive on their own. There is a 70 percent survival rate for the chicks. Emperor penguins can live for 20 to 30 years.

⬇ Emperor penguin chicks group together to form a creche.

King Penguins

King penguins breed on the islands surrounding Antarctica and have two breeding cycles over three years. Like emperor penguins, the males incubate the eggs on top of their feet. King penguins live in huge colonies on slopes close to the beach. The colonies are occupied throughout the year by either adults or chicks.

Huddling

Male emperor penguins huddle together to **conserve** their body heat while they are incubating the eggs. They change places often, taking turns standing on the edges of the creche.

Whales

Whales are mammals. They live in the ocean but must surface to breathe oxygen.

The whale family is divided into toothed whales and baleen whales (whales without teeth). Whales from both of these groups are found in Antarctic waters.

Toothed Whales

Toothed whales have sharp teeth and one blowhole. Their teeth help them to catch large **prey**. Most toothed whales feed on fish and squid, and sometimes eat seabirds, penguins, and seals. Sperm whales and killer whales are types of toothed whales.

Adaptation

Whales are well adapted to Antarctic waters because they have a layer of fat, called blubber, under their skin which provides insulation against the cold.

Sperm Whales

Sperm whales have massive, square-shaped heads. Female sperm whales live in big groups with their young calves. They weigh up to 33 tons (30 metric tons).

Killer or Orca Whales

Killer, or orca, whales spend their lives in small family groups called pods. They are fierce hunters and hunt **cooperatively** to trap seals, penguins, and other small whales. They weigh up to 9 tons (8 metric tons).

◀ Sperm whales are toothed whales. They hunt mostly fish and squid and can dive to incredible depths.

Baleen Whales

Baleen whales do not have teeth. They are filter feeders. They feed by straining plankton from the water using comb-like fringes of baleen, which hang from their upper jaw. Baleen whales also have two blowholes next to each other. Blue whales and humpback whales are types of baleen whales.

▲ Humpback whales make beautiful, soothing sounds under the water.

Humpback Whales

Humpbacks feed in groups as large as 25 whales. They eat krill and weigh up to 34 tons (31 metric tons).

▲ Blue whales can eat 2.2 tons (2 metric tons) of krill a day.

Blue Whales

Blue whales are the largest animals in the world. In the past, they were nearly hunted to **extinction**. Today, there are very low numbers of blue whales in the oceans surrounding Antarctica. They eat mainly krill and weigh up to 150 tons (136 metric tons).

Whaling

In the eighteenth and nineteenth centuries, many species of whale were nearly hunted to extinction. They were valued for their oil, bones, and baleen, which were used to make brushes and other products. Today, whales are protected by law. In 1994, the International Whaling Commission (IWC) declared an Antarctic Whale Sanctuary.

Antarctic Fish and Crustaceans

Many different kinds of sea life live in the oceans surrounding Antarctica. However, Antarctica has fewer than 200 of the 20,000 kinds of fish known in the world.

Krill

Krill are tiny crustaceans that look like shrimp. They are found in huge swarms that cover hundreds of square miles of the oceans surrounding Antarctica.

Krill are the most **abundant** animals in the world and are a vital link in the Antarctic **ecosystem**. They provide food for many different kinds of animals, including whales, seals, fish, penguins, and other birds.

The Importance of Krill

Because krill are very important in the diet of whales, seals, penguins, and other Antarctic birds, any factor that affects the numbers of krill will also have an enormous effect on these animals.

How Krill Develop

Krill **spawn** in summer. The females mature twice a season, laying 2,000 to 3,000 eggs each time. The eggs sink into deep water where they are carried by currents to the edge of the Antarctic continent. They hatch and mature. Over two or three years, they gradually rise to the surface of the ocean as adults and live for four or five years.

◄ The Antarctic species of krill is a pinkish, **translucent** shellfish that has five pairs of legs. The legs work together to make a net that filters food from the water.

Fish

Many Antarctic fish have **antifreeze** in their bodies. This substance stops their body fluids from freezing in the extremely cold temperatures.

Many fish in Antarctic waters are pale and **transparent**.

Seaweeds, sponges, corals, worms, sea anemones, and sea spiders are some of the sea animals that live on the ocean floors surrounding Antarctica.

▲ Ice fish are one type of Antarctic fish.

◀ Giant sea spiders have very small bodies. Some of their food is digested in their legs.

The Giant Sea Spider

The giant sea spider is bright orange and has 10 legs. All sea spiders have between four and 10 legs but are not related to land spiders, which have eight legs.

Overfishing

Antarctic fish are slow growing. If the numbers of Antarctic fish drop, it takes a long time for them to build up. This makes Antarctic fish very easy to overfish. Scientists work to restore the low stocks and to better manage the stocks that are still being fished.

Flying Seabirds

Some flying seabirds spend their lives on the coastal areas in Antarctica, while others stay only for the summer. Flying seabirds depend on the ocean for their food and use the coasts only for breeding.

⬆ Snow petrels have white feathers that camouflage them against the icy background.

Albatrosses

Albatrosses are the largest of the petrel family. Their long wings catch the winds and allow them to glide effortlessly at high speeds. They fly over the ocean for enormous distances. The **forceps** on their long beaks are used to hook food from the ocean.

⬆ The wandering albatross is the world's largest flying bird. It has a wingspan of more than 13 feet (4 meters).

Petrels

Petrels are the largest group of birds in Antarctica. They have tube noses and hooked bills. They spend most of the year at the edge of the pack ice and are often seen resting on icebergs. They nest in small colonies on snow-bound cliffs far inland in Antarctica. Petrels feed at sea on large squid, fish, and krill.

The Arctic Tern

The Arctic tern **migrates** farther than any other bird in the world. At the end of summer in Antarctica, it flies north to the Arctic, where summer is just beginning. Each year, the Arctic tern breeds on the coast of the Antarctic Peninsula and on sub-Antarctic islands.

Petrel Defence

The cape petrel, or pintado, is a medium-sized petrel and breeds on open cliff edges. It catches food from the ocean with its bill. Cape petrels defend their eggs and chicks by spitting bad-smelling stomach oil at their enemies.

▲ The blue-eyed cormorant will not migrate as long as it can find open water to dive for fish. These birds breed on sub-Antarctic islands and are not strong fliers.

◀ Southern skuas are often seen looking for food scraps around Antarctica's scientific bases.

Southern Skuas

Southern skuas are large gulls with hooked beaks. They are aggressive birds and are the **scavengers** of the Antarctic. They often nest near penguin and other bird colonies in order to take eggs and chicks.

Plant and Animal Life
on the Sub-Antarctic Islands

There are islands or groups of islands close to Antarctica that are called sub-Antarctic islands. The islands are windy, wet, and cold all year. Some have mountains with ice caps and snowfields, while others are completely free of ice.

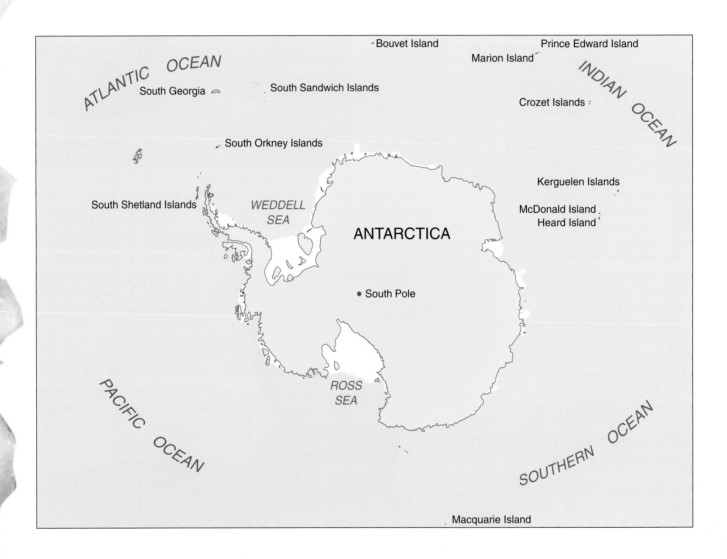

Plants

Many more plants grow on the sub-Antarctic islands with their milder climates than on Antarctica itself. Even so, no trees or shrubs grow on the islands. The tallest plants are tussock grasses, which grow 3 to 6 feet (1 to 2 meters) tall.

Seabirds

Seabirds nest on the cliffs and higher ground of many of the sub-Antarctic islands. About 35 species visit each summer, many returning to the same sites each year. They obtain their food from the sea.

Penguins on Macquarie Island

Royal penguins have a crest of black and orange feathers. They breed only on Macquarie Island. Rookeries on this island contain many thousands of birds.

⋀ Light-mantled sooty albatrosses have narrow wings and long, pointed tails that make them excellent fliers. They nest alone on high cliffs on Macquarie Island.

Macquarie Island

Australia's Macquarie Island has been a wildlife sanctuary since 1933. Prior to this time, it was a base where seals and penguins were hunted for their oil. Today there are permanent Australian National Antarctic Research Expedition bases set up on the island for scientific research.

🔻 In summer, 300,000 southern elephant seals arrive at South Georgia to breed. Huge numbers of both southern elephant and Antarctic fur seals breed in harems on sub-Antarctic islands.

27

Huskies

Huskies are strong, energetic dogs that were used in Antarctica to pull sleds for more than 100 years. Teams of huskies played an important part in the early discovery and exploration of Antarctica.

In the 1970s, dog teams were often used for **survey** work of penguin colonies on the sea shelf, but they were mainly used for recreation by **expeditioners**.

Member nations of the **Antarctic Treaty** agreed to remove all huskies because they damage the environment and disturb the wildlife. Today, huskies have been replaced completely by motor vehicles.

Husky teams were used in the Antarctic for more than 100 years.

Keeping Warm

The thick, woolly coats of huskies gave excellent protection in the cold and windy conditions of Antarctica. In a blizzard, the dogs curled up nose to tail with their backs to the wind. This kept them warm and allowed them to survive in snow as long as they had a breathing hole.

Protecting Animal and Plant Life in Antarctica

Today, through the Antarctic Treaty, nations of the world are working together to protect and conserve the plants, the animals, and the environment of Antarctica.

These nations are cooperating to achieve the delicate balance between human needs for growth and resources, and animal and plant needs for space, a pollution-free environment, and an adequate food supply.

The protection of plant and animal life in Antarctica is carried out by scientists from many different nations, who work together and share their research.

Antarctic Fact File

The Land
Antarctica is a huge, frozen continent surrounding the South Pole. It has an area of 5.5 million square miles (14.25 million square kilometers) and is the fifth largest continent.

People
No **indigenous** humans have ever lived in Antarctica. Today, scientists, support workers, and visitors stay in Antarctica for varying lengths of time.

Animals
No native land mammals live permanently in Antarctica. Seals, whales, and penguins all inhabit the waters around Antarctica. Other seabirds live in and visit Antarctica.

The largest animal that lives permanently in Antarctica is a midge, a kind of wingless fly no more than one-half inch (12 millimeters) long.

Plants
Antarctica has no trees or bushes. Only two kinds of flowering plants, and simple plants such as mosses and lichens, can grow in Antarctica.

Coldest Place on Earth
Antarctica is the coldest place on Earth. The lowest temperature ever recorded was minus 129.3 degrees Fahrenheit (minus 89.6 degrees Celsius) at the Russian base, Vostok, in July 1983.

Antarctica's annual average temperature is minus 58 degrees Fahrenheit (minus 50 degrees Celsius).

Windiest Place on Earth
Winds have been recorded at 200 miles (320 kilometers) per hour at Commonwealth Bay.

Driest Place on Earth
Precipitation, which falls mainly as snow, equals less than 5 inches (12.5 centimeters) of rain per year. This makes Antarctica a frozen desert.

Highest Continent on Earth
Antarctica is the highest of all continents. Its average **elevation** is 7,546 feet (2,300 meters) above sea level.

Highest Mountain
Antarctica's highest mountain is Vinson Massif in the Ellsworth Mountain Range. It is 16,860 feet (5,139 meters) above sea level.

The Antarctic Ice Cap
The Antarctic ice cap is a thick sheet of ice which covers almost all of the continent. At its deepest, the ice is more than 14,700 feet (4,500 meters) thick.

Antarctica holds 70 percent of the world's fresh water in the form of ice.

Ross Ice Shelf
The Ross Ice Shelf is a huge, floating cliff of ice 30 to 45 miles (50 to 70 kilometers) above sea level. Along the coast, pieces break off the ice shelf and form icebergs.

Glossary

abundant   a great quantity of something

adapted   something that has changed to fit in with the surrounding conditions

Antarctic Treaty   an agreement between many countries to protect Antarctica

antifreeze   a substance that lowers the freezing point of a liquid; some fish have an antifreeze-like substance in their bodily fluids to keep them from freezing

blubber   a layer of fat beneath the skin which keeps an animal warm

breed   the coming together of a male and a female to produce young

conserve   to save

cooperatively   where each one in the group helps the others

creche   a group of young penguin chicks who are left alone by their parents for short amounts of time

crustacean   an animal like a crab or shrimp which has a hard outer covering

defensive   wanting to protect something

dominant   most powerful

ecosystem   a community of living things

elevation   height

expeditioner   a person who makes a long and difficult journey

extinction   when a type of animal no longer exists

fast ice   ice which forms around the edges of the Antarctic continent

forceps   tong-like part of the beak that can hold objects tightly

habitat   the place where a group of animals lives

harem   a group of females with which a male can mate

ice floe   a sheet of floating ice

incubate   to keep eggs warm until they hatch

indigenous   having always lived in a certain place

insulator   something which keeps warmth in and cold out

invertebrate   an animal without a backbone

mammal   an animal that feeds on milk from its mother and gives birth to live young, rather than laying eggs

melt-water pond   a pond formed from ice which has melted

microscopic   tiny; can only be seen through a microscope

migrate   to travel regularly from one area to another

molt   to lose feathers which will soon be replaced by new ones

nutritious   full of very healthy substances that help the body grow well

overfishing   endangering a type of fish by catching too many of them

pack ice   large blocks of ice which form around the edges of Antarctica in winter, and which break up in spring and melt in summer

permanent   always there

precipitation   moisture that falls from the sky to Earth

predator   an animal that hunts another animal for food

prey   to hunt another animal for food; also an animal that is hunted by another animal for food

primary producer   the food source that all other animals in a community rely upon

regurgitate   to vomit up

rival   an enemy that wants what you have

rookery   an area where large numbers of penguins gather together

rudder   the part of a ship that is used for steering

scavenger   an animal that searches through garbage for food

South Pole   the southernmost end of Earth

spawn   to lay eggs

species   types

sub-Antarctic island   an island that lies in the warmer waters that surround Antarctica

survey   to study; to find out certain information

territory   an area that a person or animal protects as their own

translucent   transmitting light as if through frosted glass

transparent   transmitting light as if through clear glass

Index

Title VI

FY 2004